Copyright © 2005 by Mary F. Pecci

First Edition

ISBN 978-0-943220-14-7

Distributed by:

PECCI EDUCATIONAL PUBLISHERS
www.onlinereadingteacher.com
sales@onlinereadingteacher.com

Other Books by Mary F. Pecci

At Last! A Reading Method for EVERY Child! - NEW SIMPLIFIED EDITION
At Last! A Reading Method for EVERY Child! - READING SPECIALIST EDITION
Why Johnny Ain't Never Gonna Read (A Challenge to the Nation)
How to Discipline Your Class for Joyful Teaching
5 Steps to Save Our Schools

Pecci Reading Series	**Super Seatwork**
Pre-Primer I	Letter-Recognition
Pre-Primer II	Color Words
Pre-Primer III	Number Words
Primer	Content Areas
1^1 Reader	Phonic Grab Bag
Super Spelling	Linguistic Exercises
Book One	Word Skills

This Pre-Primer is designed to be used in conjunction with:
At Last! A Reading Method for EVERY Child!

ACKNOWLEDGMENTS

This reading series is dedicated to my beloved brother, Dr. Ernest F. Pecci, and his remarkable daughter, Diana Pecci La Brecque, who set this project into motion by saying those magic words, "Yes! You CAN do it!"

Sincere appreciation also goes to my sister, Marguerite Pecci Kelley, for her story suggestions and for always being on call to backboard ideas.

And a very special thanks goes to June Triesch, quintessential Kindergarten teacher, who retired on her 80th birthday, about whom such teachers it has been written, "God doesn't have hands; He uses the teacher's hands," for her constant faithfulness over the years as dearest friend and mentor.

Teacher's Guide

Pages 49 - 52

Vocabulary Word List - p. 49

Word-for-Word Dialogue
between Teacher and Student - p. 50 - 52

In this reader, 25 words are formally introduced. However, reading vocabulary will not be limited to these 25 words because students will be acquiring independent decoding skills as they progress through this reader. This reader serves only as a springboard, from which students will be able to read *any* material on (and in most cases above) their academic level.

Hi, I am Ken.

Hi, John.
See the 🚗.
Come and play.

Hi, Ken.
I see the 🚗.
I can come and play.

Hi, I am Meg.

Hi, Pam.
See the 🪢.
Come and play.

Hi, Meg.
I see the 🪢.
I can come and play.

Get the Ball

See Bo Bo run, Ken.

Bo Bo can run and get the ball.

Run, Bo Bo, run.

Run and get the ball.

Run, run, run.

See Bo Bo jump, Ken.

Bo Bo can jump and get the ball.
See Bo Bo jump.

I see Bo Bo jump, John.
Bo Bo can jump and get the ball.
Go, Bo Bo, go!

Oh, oh.

See the ball go down.
Get the ball, Bo Bo.

Run and get the ball.
Run, run, run.
Run and get the ball.

Oh, oh.

Look at Bo Bo, Ken.
See Bo Bo and the .

Come, Bo Bo, come.
Now, run and get the ball.
Run and get the ball, Bo Bo.

The Cat

Come, Scratch, come.

Come to Pam.
See the big .

Come, Scratch, come.
Come to Pam now.
Come, Scratch, come.

Scratch! Scratch!
Come to Pam.
See the big .

Come to Pam now.
Come, Scratch, come.
Come to Pam now.

Sam, see Scratch run.

Sam, get Scratch.
Run and get that cat.

Get that cat now.
Get that cat now.
Run, run, run.

Oh, Sam.

Look at Scratch.
See Scratch now.
Oh, see that cat.

Come to Pam, Scratch.
Come to Pam now.

The Dog and the Cat

Come, Bo Bo, come.

Do not get Scratch
Do not get the cat.

Come now, Bo Bo.
Do not do that.
Do not do that

Come Bo Bo, come.

Do not do that.
Come to John.

Come to Kim, Bo Bo.
Do not get that cat.
See the cat run.

Now see the cat, Kim.

Get down, Bo Bo!
Get down!

Do not do that.
The cat is up the big  .
Now the cat can not get down.

Look at John go up up, up.
John can get the cat down.
John can get the cat down.

Now go, Bo Bo, go!
Do not do that.
Do not get the cat.

The ⛵

Look at this ⛵ , Ken.

This ⛵ can not go.

I can not get this ⛵ to go.

Go, ⛵ , go.

Go, go, go!

This ⛵ can not go.

See this, Meg.

This can get the to go.

This can get the to go.

The can go with this.

The can go with this.

This can get the to go.

Do this, Meg.

Do this to the .

Do this to the .

The can go with this.

I can do this, Ken.

I can do this with the .

Now the ⛵ can go, Meg.
Look at the ⛵ go.
The ⛵ can go with the 🥄 .

This is fun, Ken.
The ⛵ can go with the 🥄 .
Now I can play with the ⛵ .

Play Ball

I want to play ball, John.
I want to play ball.

Come and play ball, John.
Come and play with this ball.
Come and play with this ball.

I want to play ball, Sam.
I want to play ball.

See the ball go to John.
See the ball go to John.

Sam and John play ball.
This is fun.

Look at this.
The ball can go to John.

Run and get the ball, John.
Run and get the ball.

This is fun.
This is fun to play ball.

Run and get the ball, John.
Run and get the ball.

Oh, Sam.
Look at this.
This is not a ball.
I want to play with a ball.
I do not want to play with this ⬡ .

The 🌸🌸

See the 🌸🌸 , Ken.

I want to get a 🌸 .

I want to get a 🌸 too, John.

Come, Ken.

We can get a 🌸 .

We can get a 🌸 now.

See Ken and John, Meg.
See Ken and John with the .
We want a too.

Come, Meg.
We can get a too.
We can get a too.

See the , Meg.

I do want a , Meg.

I do want a too, Kim.

Come, Meg.

We can get a .

We can get a too.

Oh, Kim.

Look at Bo Bo.
That dog wants a 🍪 .
That dog wants a 🍪 too.

Come, Bo Bo, come.
Come and get a 🍪 too.

The 🪢

We want to play 🪢 .

We want Ken and Sam to help.

Come, Meg.

We can get Ken and Sam to help.

Ken and Sam can help with this 🪢 .

We do not want to play .
We want to play with the   .
We can not play now.

Ken can not help with the .
Sam can not help with the .
Ken and Sam want to play in the .

Ken and Sam are in the .
We want to get help with the .

See the , Meg.
We can do this with the .

Come, Meg, come.
The can help.

Now we can play ↷, Meg.

The 🌳 can help.

Ken and Sam do not want to play.
Ken and Sam are in the 🏠 .

This is fun, Pam.
Jump up and down.

Look at This

Look at this, Kim.
This is my pet.
This is my pet, Scratch.
Scratch is my cat.

Oh, Pam.
I want to do that too.

Look Pam.
Look at this.
This is my pet.
This is my pet, Bo Bo.
Bo Bo is my dog.

Scratch and Bo Bo are fun to play with.

See this, Kim.
I can do this.

Oh, my!

See that, Pam.
I can do that.

Oh, my!

This is fun to do!

Oh, my! Look at that!
John and Sam are in the .
John did this
Sam did that.

John and Sam are not fun to play with.
Oh, my!
Look at that!

The Big Car

Hi, Ken.
I want to go to the .
I want to go with my ball.

My big car can help, Sam.
Get on my big car.
Get on, get on.

See that, Sam.
My car did help.
Look! This is the 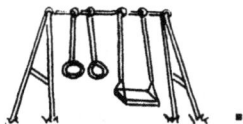 .

Now, get off, Sam.
Get off my big car.
Get off, get off.

Hi, Ken.
I want to go to the 🏪 .
I want to go now with my big 👜 .

My big car can help, Meg.
Get on my big car.
Get on, get on.

This is the , Meg.
My big car did help.
Now get off, get off.

On and off.
On and off.
This car is fun!

Meg Can Help

Look in the , Meg.
Get my .
My are in the .

I want to see my .
Get my now.

I see the .
The are in the .
I can help.

Come, Meg, come.
Come with my .
Meg can help.

Oh, oh.

I see a 〔✉〕 on the ⟋⟋⟋⟋ .

A 〔✉〕 is down on the ⟋⟋⟋⟋ .

A 〔✉〕 is down on the ⟋⟋⟋⟋ .

I did not get that 〔✉〕 .

I did not get that 〔✉〕 .

Oh my! Oh my!
Look at that dog!

Did the dog get the 〔 ▱ 〕 ?
The dog did get the 〔 ▱ 〕 .

Come, Bo Bo, come.
Bo Bo can help too.

My Pet

See my pet dog, Ken.
A pet is fun to play with.

See my pet cat, Meg.
A pet is fun to play with.

Bo Bo and Scratch are fun.

I do not want Bo Bo to get on my car.
I do not want Scratch to get on my car.

Bo Bo, do NOT get on that car.

Scratch, do NOT get on that car.

Oh, oh! Look!

The pet dog is on my car.

The pet cat is on my car.

Bo Bo and Scratch are on my car!

We do not want the dog and the cat to do that.

Get off the car, Bo Bo!

Get off the car, Scratch!

Come, Bo Bo, come to John.
Come, Scratch, come to Pam.

Get off the car.
Get off the car NOW.
Off, off, off!
Now, now, now!

Oh, my! Oh my!

Vocabulary Word List

<table>
<tr><td>

</td></tr>
</table>

* Introduce the "**all**" Sight Family beforehand.

** A Word Card is not needed for this word.

*** Introduce the "**oo**" Sight Family beforehand.

**** Introduce "**Y**" on the end says "**I**" beforehand.

***** Introduce the "**ar**" Sight Family beforehand.

Word-for-Word Dialogue

Reminder:

---

1. Write a list of the words to be introduced that day for the assigned pages, as illustrated on p. 99-101 in *At Last!*.

2. Introduce the words as scripted below.

3. Review the Word List as per the NOTE on top of p. 112 of *At Last!*.

4. Put the words introduced on flashcards and review them each day *before* introducing new words. (No word cards are needed after the Pre-Primers.)

5. Reinforce words with the Word Reinforcement activities on p. 135-140 in *At Last!* and apply the Pre-Requisite skills reinforcement activities to words.

Now, you are ready to begin!

Following is the word-for-word dialogue between teacher and student for introducing every word in this reader:

<u>Pages 1 - 4</u>

Teacher:		**Student:**

Ken -   This boy's name is "Ken."
          What's the clue?   K e n

See -   Open your eyes and you can -   S e e
          What's the clue?   S e e

(**Note:** As a general rule, it is advisable to introduce both the capital and lower-case forms of each word, when applicable. Ex. See, see.)

Meg -   This girl's name is "Meg."
          What's the clue?   M e g

<u>Pages 5 - 8</u>

NOTE: Introduce the Sight Family "**all**" <u>during the Phonic Period</u> before introducing the word "Ball."

Get -   When you go to the store, what will you -   g e t
          What's the clue?   g e t

Ball -   Underline A-L-L.   a l l
          What's the Sight family?   a l l
          What's the word?   b a l l

Run -   When you're in a hurry, you don't walk, you -   r u n
          What's the clue?   r u n

	Teacher:	**Student:**
Cat -	My pet is a - What's the clue?	C a t <u>C</u> a t
to -	This word is "to," as in "Come <u>to</u> me now." What's the clue?	 t o

| **Do -** | What am I going to -
 What's the clue? | D o
 <u>D</u> o |
| **not -** | Can you do this? No, you can -
 What's the clue? | n o t <br> n <u>o</u> t |

this -	You can't have that, but you can have - What's the clue?	t h i s <u>t h i s</u>
with -	I'm going to the store. Do you want to come - What's the clue?	w i t h <u>w</u> i <u>t h</u>
fun -	Playing games is lots of - What's the clue?	f u n f <u>u n</u>

| **want -** | How many cookies do you -
 What's the clue? | w a n t
 <u>w</u> a <u>n t</u> |
| **a -** | This word is "A," as in "I need <u>a</u> pencil."
 What's the clue? |
 <u>a</u> |

> (**Note:** Use the long "a" sound to avoid introducing
> variant sounds of this vowel. However, explain
> that it is usually pronounced "uhh" when alone.)

NOTE: Introduce the Sight Family "**oo**" during the Phonic Period before introducing the word "too."

| **We -** | This word is "we," as in "<u>We</u> want to get a cookie."
 What's the clue? |
 w <u>e</u> |
| **too -** | Underline O-O.
 What's the Sight family?
 What's the word? | <u>o o</u>
 o o <br> t o o |

	Teacher:	**Student:**
want -	We had this word before. Can you read it?	w a n t
wants -	If you add "s," what's the word?	w a n t s
	Underline the "s."	w a n t <u>s</u>

<u>Pages 29 - 32</u>

help -	When you're in danger, you yell -	h e l p
	What's the clue?	<u>h e l p</u>
in -	The cat went out, and then he came back -	i n
	What's the clue?	<u>i n</u>
are -	This word is "are," as in "We <u>are</u> having fun."	
	What's the clue?	a <u>r</u> e

<u>Pages 33 - 36</u>

NOTE: Introduce "Y" on the <u>end</u> says "I" before introducing the word "my."

my -	This word is "my," as in "This is <u>my</u> pet."	
	What's the clue?	m <u>y</u>
	Yes, "Y" on the <u>end</u> says "I."	
pet -	It is fun to play with my -	p e t
	What's the clue?	<u>p</u> <u>e</u> t
did -	I know what you -	d i d
	What's the clue?	<u>d i d</u>

<u>Pagas 37 - 40</u>

NOTE: Introduce the Sight Family "**ar**" <u>during the Phonic Period</u> before introducing the word "car."

Car -	Underline A-R.	C <u>a r</u>
	What's the Sight family?	a r
	What's the word?	C a r
on -	Please turn the light -	o n
	What's the clue?	<u>o</u> <u>n</u>
off -	Now, please turn the light -	o f f
	What's the clue?	<u>o</u> <u>f</u> <u>f</u>

<u>Pages 41 - 44</u>
(Absorption Story)

<u>Pages 45 - 48</u>
(Absorption Story)

* * * * * * * * * * * * * * * * * * *

www.ingramcontent.com/pod-product-compliance
Lightning Source LLC
Chambersburg PA
CBHW071643040426
42452CB00009B/1749